Legion of Michael:

Defending the Flock

A Comprehensive Manual for
Protecting Houses of Worship

By
Paul G. Markel, CPS

Legion of Michael:

Defending the Flock

A Comprehensive Manual for
Protecting Houses of Worship

By
Paul G. Markel, CPS
(Certified Protection Specialist)

"Praise be to the Lord my Rock, who trains my hands for war, my fingers for battle." Psalm 144:1

Warrior's Prayer

Lord, I come before you seeking the strength and skill to overcome my enemies.

Grant me I pray, the wisdom to recognize evil, the courage to confront it, and the strength to destroy it.

In Jesus name I pray, amen.

Foreword

"Bring your gun to church." is a simple piece of advice offered after almost every attack on a house of worship. While a handgun is an effective tool for stopping lethal threats, merely *having a gun* is not a deterrent for evil and it does you little good to have a gun if your first indication of trouble is someone else's gun pointed in your face.

We could take the advice of the weak and slavish and "declare" our churches to be "gun free zones". We could even post shiny plastic signs by the entrances and put a memorandum in our official church operating policy. Of course, it was illegal for the monster in Sutherland Springs, Texas to bring a gun into a church, but he did it anyway. It was illegal for him to murder twenty-six people and wound twenty more, nevertheless, he did it, regardless of the illegality of his actions. The State Law prohibiting firearms in churches did not save the lives of those twenty-six people.

Conversely, when a deranged man produced a gun and opened fire inside a church in White Settlement, Texas two years after the aforementioned incident, the outcome was much different. An armed member of the Church Security Team, Jack Wilson, swiftly drew his sidearm and stopped the maniac before he could continue. In White Settlement, two innocent people lost their lives, and hundreds were spared.

Texas State Attorney General, Ken Paxton commented on the White Settlement attack and said, "This church responded in seconds and it saved the lives of potentially over 200 people. They are the model for what other churches and places of business should focus on."

The Governor of Texas, Greg Abbott later awarded Jack Wilson the Governor's Medal of Courage. "When faced with an evil that few of us will ever comprehend, Jack Wilson responded with strength, bravery, and with love for those in the church that day," said Governor Abbott. "The courage in his actions cannot be understated, and Jack is not only a hero to the

West Freeway Church of Christ — he is a hero to the entire state of Texas."

Introduction

Introduction

For those unfamiliar with my work, allow me a moment to explain just how a person becomes a Certified Protection Specialist and offer some reasoning as to why you should take my advice. Afterall, it is only fair for the reader to be apprehensive, given the multitude of "experts" popping up on the Internet each day.

When I was sixteen or seventeen years old, I read an article in a magazine about a Bodyguard School in Aspen, Colorado. The magazine was "Gung Ho: The Magazine for the International Military Man". Inside the pages I read an in depth piece about Executive Security International, a school for bodyguards operating in the Rocky Mountains. A couple of years later, after seeing numerous ads for ESI in various magazines, I mailed a $5.00 money order to ESI to pay the price for their catalog.

A couple of weeks after receiving the catalog, an impressive item, particularly to an eighteen year old man full of testosterone, I received a phone call from a representative from

Executive Security International. The man, David, offered to answer my questions and asked me about myself, my aspirations, why I ordered the catalog, etc. The sales pitch worked and David convinced me to apply for the payment program.

David explained how ESI worked. First you would receive their home study material; a huge three-ring binder and several books. (This was long before the Internet) The student was required to complete the included tests and mail them back to ESI for grading. Only after all of the home study material was completed would the student be ready for their two week residency training course.

After about six months, I had completed all the reading and testing. David regularly phoned to discuss my progress. He kept me motivated, coached me along and then set up my date for the residency portion. The Resident Training part of the program was held in Aspen, Colorado. Students would all stay in a hotel called the Mountain Chalet.

I was 19 years old when I booked the flight that would take me from Cleveland, Ohio, to

Denver and finally to Aspen, Colorado. It was quite an adventure for a young man. During the next two weeks I would encounter some of the best training and finest instructors that I would ever know.

Harvey "Jack" McGeorge was a former Secret Service agent and previous United States Marine. Jack had an encyclopedic knowledge of almost every aspect of providing professional protection, as well as the technical aspects that the job required.

John S. Farnam, another United States Marine Corps veteran, law enforcement officer, and superb instructor, was the primary teacher for the firearms portion of training at ESI. While I had no way of understanding it at the time, I would be participating in firearms training that was decades ahead of almost all other shooting education available.

The residency training for ESI was intense. Ten to twelve hour training days were the norm. There were no days off, since time was of the essence. When I departed Aspen and returned home I was extremely excited and motivated. I felt that I drank from the fountain of knowledge.

But, and this is a big but, I was far too young to be taken seriously. Regardless of the education and training, no company was ever going to hire a 19 year old to provide professional security.

An older, wiser acquaintance, sensing my frustration, gave a piece of advice. "Why don't you join the Army and get some experience, then try again in a few years." Well, I was not about to join the Army, but the United States Marine Corps was a perfect fit for me.

During my four years of active duty service, I attended basic training, Infantry School, Sea School and became a member of the Marine Detachment aboard the USS Forrestal, an aircraft carrier. The primary mission of the MarDet was to provide security for the nuclear weapons aboard the vessel. Nuclear Weapons Security is naturally a very serious business and required special training. After two years on the Forrestal, I returned to the Marine Corps Infantry and ended up seeing front line combat during what would become the first Gulf War.

In 1993, I returned to Aspen and Executive Security International for another two week residency training program. This course focused on Intelligence Gathering and Investigation. I was reunited with Jack McGeorge and he became a mentor to me. By December of 1993 I was employed full-time as a professional bodyguard and that career would take me all over the United States, as well as overseas.

Chapter 1 Why Michael?

"Then war broke out in heaven. Michael and his angels fought against the dragon, and the dragon and his angels fought back. But he was not strong enough, and they lost their place in heaven. The great dragon was hurled down—that ancient serpent called the devil, or Satan, who leads the whole world astray. He was hurled to the earth, and his angels with him." Revelations 12:7-9

Who is Michael?

Michael the archangel is described in the Holy Bible, in the books of Daniel, Jude, and Revelation, as a warrior angel who engages in spiritual combat. The word archangel means "angel of the highest rank."

Most angels in the Bible are portrayed as messengers, but Michael is described in all three books as contending, fighting, or standing against evil spirits and principalities (Daniel 10:13; 21; Jude 1:9; Revelation 12:7). It is difficult to find a full picture of any angel, however the two who are named specifically are Michael and Gabriel. Scripture only gives us hints of their movements during human events, but it is safe to say that Michael the archangel is a powerful being.

It is truly fitting that we humans would use the example of the archangel Michael as we prepare ourselves to contend with very real and ever present evils and dangers that are a constant reality here on Earth.

The archangel Michael is also acknowledged as the patron saint of combat medics, policemen, and soldiers. Michael is officially recognized as the patron saint to watch over the US Army's 82nd Airborne Division and all paratroopers. If Michael can give his attention to paratroopers, he can bless and inspire the actions of those dedicated to protecting the innocent lives of the Lord's flock.

Chapter 2 Strength of Purpose

Greater love hath no man than this, that a man lay down his life for his friends.
-John 15:13

Before we dive into the specifics and details of providing professional security, we must first build a solid foundation. We must build our house on the rock, not upon the sand.

The primary purpose of the Legion of Michael is to defend the innocent against the attacks of evil men. There are many ways in which we will accomplish this task, but we must always hold firm to this foundational principle.

God has blessed many of us with the physical and mental abilities to be the protectors of those who cannot, for whatever reason, defend themselves from vicious evil. It would be sinful and shameful for those who have the ability to be the defenders to stand idly by while evil has its way.

I have been a Christian my entire life, thanks to God who blessed me with faithful parents. As I grew to adulthood and began to commune with warriors; strong men with the desire to defend their nation, communities, and families, I found many of them were not faithful, at least from a Christian sense of the word. They were faithful to the Corps and to their nation, but not to God.

Examining this situation closely, I discovered what I believed to be two primary misconceptions and misunderstandings by these strong men about what it means to be a faithful Christian.

One of the misunderstandings is the prime narrative from the elites in Hollywood, that is, all Christians are hypocrites. Both on television and in the movies, Christian people are portrayed as ignorant, backwoods, racists at best or two-faced hypocrites at worst. I knew this not to be true, but that is the story Hollywood pedals to the masses.

The other, as possibly the biggest turnoff to warriors about Christianity, is the misconception that in order to be a Christian, you must be weak, subservient, and allow evil men to trample you. Once more, I knew this to be a lie. Nonetheless, the perception that a Christian man must act in a slavish or cowardly manner is an instant no sale to men who have devoted their lives to the warrior pursuits.

The first myth of the ignorant, racist, hypocrite is dispelled by setting the example. However, the idea that Christians are somehow duty-bound by their faith to be weak, subservient, and even slavish must be refuted with scripture and actual Church doctrine.

First of all, the prime misconception is that the 6th commandment is supposed to read "Thou Shall Not Kill" and that means no killing of any kind, ever, or you have committed sin. The Ten Commandments were passed down in Hebrew. The translation from Hebrew to English is "Thou shall not commit murder". Murder is the unlawful and unjust killing of a human. Kill is a super generic term. We kill mosquitoes and rodents because they are a nuisance and carry disease. We kill cattle, hogs and chickens so we can eat them and stay alive. The ancient Hebrews killed animals in sacrifice to God. There are innumerable times when killing is necessary and proper.

People who would claim that you cannot shoot a home invader or an armed robber if you are a Christian, because it is a sin, do not understand the difference between "kill" and "murder". More often it is not that they don't understand, it is that they are behaving in an intellectually lazy manner.

In the book of Psalms 144:1, King David gives thanks to God, *"Praise be to the Lord my Rock, who trains my hands for war, my fingers for battle."*

In the book of Ecclesiastes 3:1-8, King Solomon, a man who God granted greater wisdom than any person who has lived or will ever live, wrote; *"There is an appointed time for everything. And there is a time for every event under heaven— A time to give birth and a time to die; A time to plant and a time to uproot what is planted. A time to kill and a time to heal; A time to tear down and a time to build up. A time to weep and a time to laugh; A time to mourn and a time to dance. A time to throw stones and a time to gather stones; A time to embrace and a time to shun embracing. A time to search and a time to give up as lost; A time to keep and a time to throw away. A time to tear apart and a time to sew together; A time to be silent and a time to speak. A time to love and a time to hate; A time for war and a time for peace."*

There are people who would say that the Old Testament does not matter, that only the New Testament of Christ is valid. Jesus Christ, our perfect example, said in Matthew 10:34 *"Do not think that I came to bring peace on the earth; I did not come to bring peace, but a sword."* Christ also advises in Luke 22:36 *"But now, whoever has a money belt is to take it along, likewise also a bag, and whoever has no sword is to sell his coat and buy one."*

Many will say that Christ was speaking metaphorically and that he never would advise his followers to carry a genuine sword or to engage in combative or violent behavior. To those people I would ask them to ponder the following.

In Matthew 21, Jesus cleansed the temple *"And Jesus went into the temple of God, and cast out all them that sold and bought in the temple, and overthrew the tables of the moneychangers, and the seats of them that sold doves, And said unto them, It is written, My house shall be called the house of prayer; but ye have made it a den of thieves."*

Christ did not meekly or subserviently ask politely for the money changers to relocate. He **drove them out**. In John Chapter 2 it reminds us, *"And when he had made a scourge of small cords, he drove them all out of the temple, and the sheep, and the oxen; and poured out the changers' money, and overthrew the tables;".*

That story is so important that it is included in all four books of the Gospel. Christ found his Father's house being used as a den of thieves and became angry. So angry in fact that he fashioned a scourge (whip) out of cords and drove the money changers out. In common parlance, he whipped their asses. Does that sound like the actions of a weak, slavish, subservient person?

What is the lesson here? I believe this story was provided for us, times four, in order that we may understand that righteous anger is not a sin. Anger is an emotion that should be used to motivate us to take corrective action.

Regarding the Legion of Michael, if an evil man threatens grave harm to an innocent person, it is righteous and correct to be angered by that situation. That anger motivates us to take steps to halt, or stop, that threat.

Some of you may have to contend with, and educate, the intellectually lazy or the woefully misinformed. In addition to the references above, please take note of the official doctrines of both the Lutheran and Roman Catholic Churches in regard to self-defense and the taking of human life.

(*Beware of Internet research. Political correctness has infected even the church. The result is the alteration of original texts to suit modern culture. The best sources are actual books written and published before the PC revision.)

Lutheran Catechism

"Life may be taken without breaking the fifth commandment *(*author's note: Roman Catholics and Lutherans number the 10 Commandments differently)* in self-defense, in the public defense (nation or community), in executing a judicial sentence, and by unavoidable accident."

Roman Catholic Catechism

2263 The legitimate defense of persons and societies is not an exception to the prohibition against the murder of the innocent that constitutes intentional killing. "The act of self-defense can have a double effect: the preservation of one's own life; and the killing of the aggressor. .. The one is intended, the other is not."

2264 Love toward oneself remains a fundamental principle of morality. Therefore it is legitimate to insist on respect for one's own right to life. Someone who defends his life is not guilty of murder even if he is forced to deal his aggressor a lethal blow.

If a man in self-defense uses more than necessary violence, it will be unlawful: whereas if he repels force with moderation, his defense will be lawful. .. Nor is it necessary for salvation that a man omit the act of moderate self-defense to avoid killing the other man, since one is bound to take more care of one's own life than of another's.

What did Pope John Paul II have to say about self-defense?

Pope John Paul II addressed the issue of taking human life in the EVANGELIUM VITAE in 1995 when he stated "Moreover, legitimate defence can be not only a right but a grave duty for someone responsible for another's life, the common good of the family or of the State. Unfortunately, it happens that the need to render the aggressor incapable of causing harm sometimes involves taking his life. In this case, the fatal outcome is attributable to the aggressor whose action brought it about, even though he may not be morally responsible because of a lack of the use of reason."

On a personal note, I was privileged to lead a team of security personnel during the visit of Pope John Paul II during the World Youth Day event that took place during the summer of 1993 in Denver, Colorado. It saddens me that the massive shoes John Paul left have gone unfilled in the time since his passing.

Now that we have laid the foundation for legitimate defense of the innocent, upto and including the taking of human life, we are ready to move on and discuss the how-to portion of providing professional security.

Finally, be strong in the Lord and in his mighty power. Put on the full armor of God, so that you can take your stand against the devil's schemes.
Ephesians 6:10-11

Chapter 3 Firearms, Ammunition, and Holsters

When a strong man, fully armed, guards his own house, his possessions are safe Luke 11:21

As mentioned at the outset, "bring your gun to church" is not an effective security strategy. Nonetheless, a firearm is an indispensable tool for self-defense and the defense of innocent life. The carrying of a firearm in public, and the employment of said arm around the innocent, is not something to be taken lightly. Owning a gun does not make you any more qualified to use it during the gravest extreme than owning a guitar makes you a musician.

Men often spend an inordinate amount of time focusing on the object that is the gun and woefully inadequate amount of time training and practicing with that gun. When I attended ESI and took part in the firearms portion, that segment included four, twelve hour days of intensive training. How many people who desire to simply "carry a gun" to church have undergone 48 hours of supervised firearms training?

Training and practice, for our discussion, are not interchangeable terms. Training is a formal exercise that takes place under the watchful eye or eyes of a skilled and experienced instructor or instructors. Practice is what you do after you have undergone training.

Think about our guitar analogy. We take lessons from a music instructor to teach us how to, and what to, practice. After we leave that guitar instructor, we are expected to go home and practice what we were taught.

Choosing a Sidearm

There are thousands of guns available to the American gun buyer, however, for our purposes, we will focus on the defensive handgun. No one wants to attend a church service where men with rifles are staged at the entrances. Despite the fact that rifles are better fight stoppers than handguns, we should be discreetly carrying our guns.

Pocket pistols and tiny handguns are comforting, but the reality of the matter is that small guns are difficult to master and hold a finite amount of ammunition. The preferred concealed pistol for the Legion of Michael will be nearly identical to that which a police officer would carry on a daily basis.

American men tend to view their firearms choices as a pseudo-religion. We wrap far too much of our egos around our choice of maker.

Let's lay out a few criteria for the handgun;

#1   Reliability - Your pistol must be as close to 100 percent reliable as the hand of man can make it. If you experience frequent stoppages, more than one per 500 rounds, your gun is not reliable.   You will note that reliability was placed before accuracy.

#2   Functionality - Can you make the handgun work immediately, using only your strong (dominant) hand or your support (non-dominant) hand? The more external controls on the gun, the greater the amount of time that will be required to master that gun. That is simply mechanics. Standard transmission cars have their place, but they take far more time to learn and master than automatic transmission cars.

If your choice of handgun has multiple external controls or is purpose built to be used by right handers or left handers, you are handicapping yourself. No, I don't care how much of your ego you have invested in that gun.

#3   Accuracy - Modern firearms are built with more inherent accuracy than most shooters will ever be able to realize. The manufacturing processes have allowed gun makers to produce firearms that are better built, reliable, and accurate than at any time during our history. There is inherent accuracy that is built into the gun and there is practical accuracy that comes from the hands of the operator.

Yes, you must test your handgun to ensure that the bullets are striking where the sights are indexed. Keep in mind, most accuracy issues (99 percent) come from the user, not the gun.

#4   Caliber - The most practical and useful defensive caliber is 9x19mm. This is not World

War II where GI Joe was relying on 230 full metal jacket ammunition. Modern 9mm Parabellum, NATO, or Luger (they are all the same) ammunition is lightyears ahead of that which was available even twenty years ago.

If your personal preference is for another caliber, so be it. That gun still must pass the first three criteria tests outlined above.

A good friend and firearm training mentor, Ken Hackathorn, advised during his training program that gun carriers should not rely on the "average number of rounds fired" statistics that are floating around.

Ken reminded his students that there are "shootings" and there are "gunfights" and that they are not the same. A shooting is when one person had a gun. In that case the average is about three shots fired. A gunfight is when all parties have guns. The average amount of rounds fired by parties in a gunfight are all the rounds the gun holds.

Police officers who are involved in legitimate gunfights against armed opponents will, as often as not, shoot their pistols until they stop making noise (slidelock or empty mag). Yes, this obviously is not an absolute statistic, but it is very common.

Keep the following advice in mind; you are NOT penalized for having rounds left in your gun when the fight is over. If you start with fifteen rounds and only use four or five to stop the attacker(s), you still win. However, if you start with five rounds and run out before your opponent(s) does/do, the penalty you may pay is your life or the lives of innocent people.

Ammunition Choice

All ammunition manufacturers produce training ammo and defensive loads. A handgun cartridge is composed of **4 Parts**: the **case**, the projectile or **bullet**, the **primer cap**, and the **propellant** powder. When a manufacturer produces a defensive load, one that the shooter will be using to protect their life, they use premium or more expensive components.

A quality defensive load will have a controlled expansion bullet (hollow-point). These come in many varieties but all are designed to expand/open up when they strike something solid like animal tissue. The reason for this is two-fold. Expanding bullets reduce the chance of the bullet passing completely through the target and they will also potentially do more damage to the target thus reducing the number of rounds it takes to stop the threat.

*Author's Note: The Honeybadger line of defensive ammunition from Black Hills Ammunition, uses non-expanding bullets that are purpose built to provide the same type of wounding effect that traditional controlled-expansion projectiles produce.

Some of the premium components in defensive ammo include nickel (silver) cases, sealed (moisture-proof) primers, and flash-reducing propellant powder. Due to the fact that defensive ammunition is built from premium components it is naturally more expensive. In this case, you get what you pay for.

Training or practice ammunition is purposely built from less expensive components. By using less expensive components the manufacturer is able to reduce the consumer cost thus allowing you to shoot more for less money. Practice ammunition will be loaded with full metal jacket (non-expanding) or solid lead bullets and the cases will be standard brass, lacquered steel, or aluminum.

When it comes time to choose ammunition keep in mind; premium defensive ammo goes in the gun for that "just in case" moment. Less expensive training ammo is what you will take to a class or out to practice.

Your life, and the lives of those whom you have sworn to protect, deserves a genuine investment. That tool on our hip may be called upon to save a life. That is not the time for bargain shopping for the cheapest ammo you can find.

Holster Choice

As with our previous discussion of ammunition, this a serious subject upon which we have embarked, therefore, this is not the time to go bargain shopping for holsters. Your holster and belt are critical components for the armed security provider.

Like firearms, there are dozens upon dozens of makers from which to choose. That decision is yours to make, but it should be an informed decision, not one based upon emotion or cost-cutting.

Holster criteria will include;

#1   Dedicated Design - the holster must be specifically designed for the particular make and model of handgun you have chosen to carry. "One size fits most" holsters are amateur-hour and a hazard to you and others.

#2   Secure Fit - the holster should carry the gun securely so as to prevent either the gun from negligently coming out or shifting around as you go about normal activity. We are not talking about repelling from a helicopter or parachuting onto an objective. Multiple security features may be preferable for exposed duty carry, but not necessary for concealed carry. As with the firearm, the more options/controls the holster has, the higher the learning curve and the more likely the gun will not be available when you need it the most.

#3   Rigid construction - whether you are using leather, Kydex, polymer, or some combination, the holster body should be rigid enough to prevent a negligent depression of the trigger. Cheap, bargain holsters are particularly culpable in that regard.

#4   Accessible - The holster must be worn in a position that allows the user to access the gun immediately; think 2 seconds maximum draw time. We are not going to be walking around with guns in our hands. When the time comes to need the gun, we need it now, not after we engage in a strange Kabuki dance.

Drawing the holster from concealment should be practiced initially with an empty gun or a solid, plastic trainer gun. If all you are doing is draw practice, you do not need ammunition in the gun. Get comfortable with your gear to the point where it becomes a natural extension to your body and not a complicated exercise.

Belt holsters require a quality belt. No, the black or brown dress belt that you bought from the mall is not a gun belt. Dress belts are designed for fashion, not utility, and will not hold up to supporting the extra two to three pounds of gear you add to them. The good news is that every quality holster maker also makes quality belts. We have come a long way in the gun belt department. There are gun belts available now that will blend with dress clothing.

Yes, I speak from experience. The first year I was working as a bodyguard I made the mistake of trying to match a brown dress belt with a brown leather holster. The belt broke while I was on duty. Fortunately, I had a second belt with me on that contract.

Chapter 4 Choosing a Team

Two are better than one, because they have a good return for their labor:
If either of them falls down, one can help the other up. But pity anyone who falls and has no one to help them up.
Also, if two lie down together, they will keep warm. But how can one keep warm alone?
Though one may be overpowered,two can defend themselves. A cord of three strands is not quickly broken.

Ecclesiastes 4:9-12

Guns, ammo, and holsters are merely tools, inanimate objects. It is the human that acts as the operating system for the objects. That is where our team comes in.

Now is the time to consider the criteria and traits that we will look for in a member of the Legion of Michael church security team. Just like Varsity Football or Basketball, not everyone is going to make the cut for the team. This is the time to put away the childish notions of "fair" or "equal". Return to the purpose of our undertaking; direct confrontation with evil to save the lives of the innocent. Not every person in the congregation will possess the physical and mental aptitude and ability.

The most basic criteria are physical. Does the person possess the physical strength and stamina to stand on their feet before, during, and after, a church service? Do not laugh, there will be those who show interest in the position who cannot easily do that.

Hearing and vision are important factors for both observation for threats and communication between team members. Most adult men have some hearing loss to a varied degree, particularly veterans, but you need to be able hold a normal conversation and hear someone calling for help. Corrected vision is fine, but vision problems need to be correctable.

Do they have the physical ability to carry and deploy a firearm and the necessary skill to use one in the presence of innocent people? We will get into the firearm qualification details in the training section of this book. However, if they cannot pass a simple firearms qualification course, they should not be carrying one in public.

While it is not necessary for the person in question to be a professional strongman or athlete, they need to be able to move quickly on demand and, when called for, exert force onto a threat. We must assume that at some point members of the security team will have to restrain a human attacker. A man with chronic back and hip issues, who takes five minutes to climb five stairs may be motivated to serve but is not physically up to the task.

The mental or psychological qualifications for a team member are a bit more difficult to gauge than the physical. From the very beginning, Legion members must have the desire to serve their congregation and service means some personal sacrifice. Membership on the church security team is voluntary. So the rewards are less tangible than money.

The person who wants to spend all of their time telling you about how many and what kinds of guns they own is not necessarily the kind of person for your team. Yes, you need to own a firearm, but I would be far more impressed by hearing what training courses that person has attended rather than a laundry list of their favorite toys.

Along the lines of training, any person who is unwilling to volunteer their time to attend training automatically disqualifies themself. Yes, people have job and family commitments, but the person who begins by making excuses not to attend training is not serious about the mission.

People who already have life experience and training with firearms are naturally preferable. Military veterans and police officers should be ahead of the curve when it comes to physical abilities and dedication to the mission. Again, that is not an absolute.

The greatest mental attribute for a LM candidate is a willingness to learn, train, and work as a member of a team. Working as a team member requires the fortitude to park the ego, listen, and take instructions. Sadly, not all adults have the wherewithal to do that.

It is a safe bet to say that, based upon the fact that you are reading this text, you will be involved in the leadership of your church security team. Keep in mind that some, or maybe even many, of the people who you choose to be on your team will not necessarily last for long. That is okay. A new team will experience growing pains.

One of the easiest ways to determine a person's dedication is to consider their church membership history. While it is fine to accept new church members onto a team, parishioners with a long track record of church membership have already displayed their dedication to the church family. If someone is not willing to officially become a member of the congregation, how dedicated will they be to your team?

All of the above qualifications, both physical and psychological, should be on paper and written down. That way it will not appear that the qualifications are an arbitrary way for you, the leader, to exclude someone. The same rules apply to all. That way there is no impartial favoritism.

Chapter 5 Training

Instruct the wise and they will be wiser still; teach the righteous and they will add to their learning. Proverbs 9:9

You will recall our earlier discussion of Training versus Practice. Training is a structured event, led by one or more experienced instructors. Practice is something you can do on your own, at your own pace.

One of the greatest aspects of attending training is that it builds camaraderie in the team members. It is critically important that all members of the team engage in regular training together. Giving yourself, or someone else, a pass on a training class because it is too basic or redundant will erode the respect that members have for their leadership. Lead by example.

Formal training does not have to take place all the time or even monthly, but you should strive to have formal training weekends, at very least, every six months. If you can afford the time, quarterly training is a noble goal.

Firearms Training

When we mention training, the natural tendency is to think about firearms training. When it comes to training with a handgun, I would suggest that all Legion members undergo, at minimum, sixteen hours. The course should be geared around the defensive use of a handgun, not competition or recreation. Speed drills with shot timers look cool to the outside observer, but can actually be detrimental to, or at very least detract from, the martial aspect of training.

There are many schools from which to choose. Tactical Response in Tennessee is on the top of our recommended list. Any course taught by John S. Farnam is worth taking. Clint Smith and his Thunder Ranch school have a stellar reputation, as does the Gunsite Academy in Arizona. The Tactical Defense Institute in Ohio is another highly recommended school. Like John Farnam, if you can get into one of Dave Spaulding's mobile classes, do it.

The vast majority of defensive pistol classes are built around the idea of the lone defender, not a team. This is where baby steps come into play. First, make sure that everyone on your team is up to speed as an individual gun handler. When that mission is accomplished, you can move on to team based training with firearms. Regardless of where you are located, it is important that your Legion members all have a foundational, or fundamental, set of skills. For example, it may not be possible or practical for all of your team members to take a Tactical Response class together. They can take the training at different times, but still get the same thing out of it.

Regardless of the particular firearms school you choose, there absolutely must be an emphasis on the 4 Universal Firearms Safety Rules:

1) *Keep your finger straight and off the trigger* until the sights are aligned and you've made the decision to fire. This is the number one most broken safety rule. Remember, "Off target, off trigger". The trigger is not a finger rest. Casually or reflexively placing the finger

on the trigger is amateurish and the leading cause of negligent shootings.

2) *Never allow the muzzle to cover anything you are not willing to destroy*. This rule says "willing to destroy" not "intend to shoot". There is a difference. If I am loading a firearm and it's pointed at the ground, I don't intend to shoot the ground but, if somehow the gun were to discharge the projectile would not likely strike anyone. Before you point a firearm at anything ask yourself, "If the gun were to fire right now, will anyone bleed?" It's a simple Yes/No question.

3) *Treat All Guns as if they are loaded all the time*. This rule trumps the; "It's okay, it's not loaded" amateur gun handling excuse. A firearm can only be considered unloaded after it has been verified by two independent means. This could be two people checking the gun or one person inspecting the gun both visually and physically. After a negligent shooting no one ever says "I thought the gun was loaded."

4) *Know your target*, what is around it and what is beyond it. Not every bullet your fire will strike the center of your intended target and

many of those that do will pass through the target and continue to travel. Remember you own every bullet that exits your firearm. If a bullet/projectile from your firearm strikes something it should not have, you are the responsible party.

If you examine the four universal safety rules thoroughly, you will come to realize that they apply everywhere, at all times, even to include during a gunfight. Yes, the rules apply during a gunfight. There are far more things in this world that should not be shot, versus those that should be. Just because a maniac walks into your church with a gun does not mean that you can launch bullets indiscriminately all over the place. You are responsible for your actions at all times, even during a gunfight.

Medical Training

While skill with a firearm is important, there is other training that is valuable and an important part of your team's skill set. CPR and Heimlich training is a must have and it should be relatively easy to come by. However, CPR/Heimlich is where you start, not where you finish.

Every member of your team should attend a traumatic medical training course. Our Beyond the Band Aid course is sixteen hours long. Use that time line as a benchmark. Thankfully, trauma training is more readily had now than it was only a few years ago. Traumatic medical instruction should cover how to deal with genuine life-threatening emergencies, such as major bleeding, loss of an airway, and a punctured lung. In addition to carrying a firearm, every member of your team, at minimum, should have a ready-made tourniquet on their person and understand how to use it.

When you go through trauma training you will learn and understand why we do NOT do CPR on people who have gunshot wounds or any other major bleeding emergency. This kind of training is critical. Remember, you can win the gunfight and still have to deal with bleeding good guys/innocent victims. We cannot shoot the wound closed.

As for where to find Traumatic Medical training, look to the previous list of trainers and schools. The majority offer some type of trauma courses.

Physical Training

As we mentioned earlier, there may very well be a time when the best option for the security team is to go hands on with a threat. Not every problem or threat that arises will justify or warrant the use of a firearm. The old saying goes, to the man who only has a hammer, every problem is a nail. To those who only have a gun, every problem can seem like a shooting problem, but that is not the case.

Returning to our idea that members of the Legion should be physically fit and free from disabling factors, we live in a world where there is still occasion to physically control people who pose a threat to the innocent members of our congregation. From a moral and legal standpoint (discussed in detail later) you cannot pull out a gun and shoot or threaten to shoot every disorderly, argumentative, or unbalanced person who walks in the front door. Before you jump ahead, there are indeed less-than-lethal tools with which we can deal with non-lethal threats. That comes next.

There are any number of grappling classes and training gyms available. Judo and Jujitsu are the most common grappling arts available. Were I the leader of a Legion of Michael team, I would approach the local grappling instructor and explain who I was and for what I was looking. A good instructor will be able to remove the sport competition component and focus on the practical method of subject control. Our goal here is not to gain points or win trophies, but to use our tools and skills to save lives.

Less-than-Lethal Force

Less-than-Lethal force tools are those which bridge the gap between talking, empty hands, and using a firearm. Not every potential threat can be dealt with by gunfire. However, just because you cannot shoot the threat, does not mean you can ignore it.

A classic example would be a drunk or drugged up troublemaker who has entered your church. That problem must be addressed, but minus a weapon or their intent to use a weapon, you cannot legitimately use a firearm. What are you going to do?

The TASER, not a stun gun from the mall, but a genuine tool from TASER, Inc. is a tremendously effective less-than-lethal tool when employed properly. The TASER is an electronic subject control tool and the electrical impulse affects both the pain sensors and the sympathetic nervous system. In other words, it hurts, but it does not rely upon pain compliance to work. The stun gun from the mall is a pain compliance tool and is worthless on a person who is numb to pain due to alcohol or narcotics or just adrenaline.

TASER tools can be purchased perfectly legally in most parts of the United States and TASER, Inc. has training programs available. The downside with the TASER unit is that it is essentially a one shot opportunity. If you miss, the bad guy is not just going to stand still while you load a fresh cartridge.

OC or Pepper Spray is another very effective less-than-lethal use of force tool when employed properly. OC is a low end use of force that does not leave the suspect with permanent harm or damage. Decontamination is completed with a lot of water and open air. This is where your training comes into play. OC training not only teaches you how to properly use the tool, it teaches you how to decontaminate a person.

OC (Oleoresin Capsicum) is the law enforcement term for pepper spray. The downside to OC is that it is delivered as a spray. That is also why it works so well. In the close confines of a crowded church, if you must use OC, the chances are high that there will be some cross-contamination and more people will be affected than your hostile suspect. Again, OC exposure does not require a hospital trip, just a lot of cold water and a fan would be helpful.

If you do decide to use an OC product, there is a foam delivery system available that minimizes cross-contamination or overspray to the greatest extent possible. This would be a better use for a church security team who will be working indoors most of the time.

Please note, there is a huge quality difference between the pepper spray sold at the gas station or discount store and that which is sold to law enforcement. When it comes time to purchase an OC product, buy it from a police supply store. Just like the TASER, OC is perfectly legal in the vast majority of the country.

Team Building

Not all of your training activities must be of a super serious, life and death nature. As a leader, you should organize activities that foster a team building atmosphere and a spirit of camaraderie. Many of these events may be determined by what is available in your geographic area.

Some suggestions for team building training activities could be confidence courses or high rope courses. Many professional summer camps have these programs. Horseback riding and canoeing are great team builders. Overnight camping trips with survival training (Fire Starting, Water Purification, Compass Reading) built in, are good for the team. If you live up north or in the mountainous west, snowshoeing or cross country skiing are options.

The point is simply this, take the time to organize events that are both educational and enjoyable. No one wants to spend all of their time on life and death, doom and gloom scenarios. Look for a way to find balance in your Legion training activities. The most important part of the team training is the team building experience.

Chapter 6 Justifiable Use of Force

Guns, ammunition, holsters, OC, TASERs, etc, are all just objects. They are tools. Before we consider using these tools against a person or persons, we must be absolutely clear that our actions are not just morally justified, but legally justifiable as well. Fortunately, this is not as complicated or complex as many would have you to believe. The following information is taught to police officers in academies all over the United States. It has been affirmed by legal precedent all the way up to the Supreme Court.

Carrying a concealed weapon is about one thing: Personal Defense/Protection. We don't carry concealed because we're going to shoot beer cans off of a stump, we do it so that we can halt or prevent anyone from doing us harm or harming an innocent person. In all of human history, the handgun is the most effective of the "concealable" protective tools.

After we have acknowledged the fact that concealed handguns are for personal protection we must deal with the reality that, due to no fault of our own, we may be forced to shoot someone; a human.

You must be honest with yourself. Could you fire a gun at a two-legged predator if your life or the life of an innocent person was in jeopardy? Some people cannot and that's fine, but those people should not be carrying guns. We outlined the difference between killing a deadly threat and murder in the beginning of this text.

Deadly Force: "Deadly force is that force which could reasonably be expected to cause death or serious (grave) bodily harm." Death is simple to define. It means not being alive anymore. "Serious Bodily Harm" on the other hand is a bit more complex.

"Serious Bodily Harm" has been legally defined as "harm that causes or is likely to cause permanent disability or disfigurement or require prolonged hospitalization and/or rehabilitation." Scars, broken bones, and paralysis all fall into the serious bodily harm category.

By this definition you can see that being shoved, a simple punch in the nose, or a punch in the stomach would not fall into the category of Serious Bodily Harm. On the other hand, being struck in the knees with a baseball bat, though unlikely to cause death, would be considered "Serious Bodily Harm" as it would likely result in permanent or prolonged disability. The use or threatened use of deadly force is either justified by the circumstances or it is a crime (felony).

Consider this - a police officer shoots an armed robber threatening people with a gun: Justified. An armed robber shoots a police officer who is attempting to arrest them: Capital Crime/Felony. Both parties used a firearm, but the circumstances were different.

Less-than-Lethal Force: Less-than-Lethal Force is a minimal amount of force that is *unlikely* to cause death or serious bodily harm. Personal defense tools such as Pepper Spray and the TASER are good examples of Less-than-Lethal Force tools.

Deadly Force is only justified if a reasonable person would fear for their life or that of another person. In order to articulate a reasonable fear of death or serious bodily harm the following criteria must be met:

The Big 3 Checklist

Ability: Attackers use of a weapon, size, strength or number, or the victim's lack of these. When an attacker produces a weapon capable of inflicting serious bodily harm or death, that demonstrates ability.

Disparity of Force: Consider the age, sex, size, number and skill level, and weapons possessed by attacker versus victim. In regards to a disparity or demonstrable difference, the courts recognize that if the attacker has disparity in their favor (Size, Strength, Age, Sex, Number) the defender may use more force than might otherwise be needed.

For instance, the courts have ruled that if two or more persons attack a single defender, the strength in their numbers constitutes a threat of deadly force, regardless of whether or not the multiple attackers show weapons. The courts recognize that a lone defender can be crippled or killed if they are attacked by multiple persons, therefore, the single defender can be legally justified in using deadly force to stop the attack.

Another common disparity of force situation would be a young, physically fit male attacker, in the late teens or early twenties, assaulting an older man or woman. The courts do not expect a 65 year old man with a history of back problems to duke it out toe to toe with a young, fit attacker. In such a case, the 65 year old man would be legally justified in using greater force than if the two parties' age and strength were more closely matched.

Opportunity: Does the attacker have access to the victim? Can the attacker's weapon be used against the victim? Think of a contact weapon versus a firearm.

Consider this - a man standing in a parking lot holding a knife. A knife is a deadly tool, but if there is no one close by, within twenty-five feet or so, they do not have the opportunity to use it. How about a man standing at the end of your driveway with a baseball bat in his hand screaming at you? While a bat can be deadly, if he can't get to where you are, you are not justified in using deadly force, regardless of how menacing his behavior may be.

Intent (Jeopardy): Intent is demonstrated by words and/or actions made by an attacker that would lead a reasonable person to fear for their life and safety. What actions did the threat engage in that would lead a person to be in fear for their life?

The most common example would be a street mugging. A stranger produces a weapon; knife, gun, etc. and demands that you surrender your money, phone, whatever. That action is a demonstration of intent to do harm. Therefore, deadly force on the part of the defender is justified.

One Legal Example: The Mississippi State Statute defines *Justifiable Homicide…* "the killing of a human being by the act, procurement or omission of another **shall be justifiable**…when committed by any person in resisting any attempt unlawfully to kill such person or to commit any felony upon him, or upon or in any dwelling, in any occupied vehicle, in any place of business, in any place of employment or in the immediate premises thereof in which such person shall be."

A firearm is a tool that we use to stop someone from using deadly force against us. We don't try to "scare" people with guns or hope that the mere sight of the gun will cause them to flee.

You may not be required to fire your weapon, but you need to be mentally prepared to do so if the situation dictates. Do not try to bluff a violent criminal.

No Warning Shots: Only Naval Vessels are allowed to fire warning shots. You are either justified in firing a gun at someone or you are not. Keep in mind that you are responsible for every round that exits the muzzle. What goes up must come down. Warning shots are loose rounds looking for an innocent victim.

We Do Not "Shoot to Wound"*:* Again, discharging a firearm at a person constitutes deadly force, or at very least the threat of deadly force. You are either justified or you are not. You do not get extra "mercy" or "reasonable" points in court for trying to "shoot to wound".

Saying that you tried to "shoot to wound" is actually tantamount to admitting that the situation DID NOT require deadly force, but you used it anyway. That type of behavior is both reckless and negligent and will not win you favors with a judge or prosecuting attorney.

Every member of the Legion of Michael team must be thoroughly trained and educated in the justifiable use of force. Your standard operating procedures should include not only the definition of Deadly Force and the Big 3 Checklist, there also needs to be a written prohibition against the firing of warning shots or a deliberate attempt to shoot to wound.

When a deadly threat appears, we shoot it until it is no longer a threat. There is no predetermined round count for deadly force encounters. It may take one round or all the rounds that you have in your gun to stop the deadly threat from committing harm to you or innocent people. You will not know the answer to that question until the fight is over.

Armed men are always to be considered dangerous and deadly, regardless of whether or not handgun bullets have struck them. During the FBI Miami Shootout in April of 1986, Michael Platt received what doctors called a "non-survival gunshot wound" during the first minute of the gun battle. Platt went on to kill two agents and wound five others AFTER receiving that wound. Platt was not on PCP or any other narcotics. His veins were filled with adrenaline and hatred.

The purpose of that history lesson is to drive home the point that even after bad men are shot, many of them will continue in their attempt to kill you or others. You must have the intestinal fortitude to do whatever it takes to make them stop. Again, this could be one shot, like our example from White Settlement, Texas, or it could take every round you have in your gun.

Chapter 7

Standard Operating Procedures

While some folks may consider the creation of a set of Standard Operating Procedures, or SOP's, to be overkill for a small town church that has 122 members and four men on the security team, a set of SOP's is a sign of professionalism.

Also, we must assume that having a security team is not a one time thing or some fashionable trend. From the beginning we must look at the longevity of the team and consider that the team may be in place for much longer than the original members are a part of it.

The beginning of our SOP planning should be to establish a written mission statement. Be thorough, but take care not to overcomplicate the mission. There is no way you will be able to anticipate every possible scenario.

Mission Statement

A simple, straight-forward mission statement is valuable, for example;

"The mission of the Legion of Michael church security team is to provide protection for members of the congregation, staff, and visitors against any threats or harm. The innocent will be protected from those with harmful or evil intent by whatever means are deemed appropriate for the immediate situation."

That two sentence mission statement sums up the purpose of the team without getting dragged down by minutia or lengthy verbiage. Any person who reads the statement should completely understand the purpose of the church security team.

Official Church Policy for self-defense and the defense of the innocent should be included in the SOP. See the various catechisms and statements of Pope John Paul II.

The Use of Force model should be based upon the universally accepted definitions of deadly force and less than lethal force. An understanding of Ability, Opportunity, and Intent is a priority for all personnel. The Use of Force Policy model should also take into account the State Statutes for whichever jurisdiction the church happens to be in.

Incident Reports

The church attorney should either create or bless off on a standardized Incident Report form. Any activity that is out of the ordinary or requires direct attention of the security team should be documented, even if the police are not called, and even if the incident is only verbal and not physical.

Witness statement reports should be attached to all Incident Reports. These will be handwritten and copies need to be secured in the Church Office. Like tax records, incident reports should be kept for years.

Leadership and Organization

Other items to be included in the SOP book would be the makeup of the Legion of Michael team itself, as in Team Leader, Assistant Team

Leader, Training Director, etc. Also, basic requirements for admission to the team must be spelled out in writing, not just "understood". Not everyone will "understand" why they did not make the cut to be on the security team. By putting the requirements, especially training requirements, in writing, you will be far less likely to be accused of favoritism or behaving in a way that arbitrarily excludes people.

Again, the physical size of your facility and number of congregants will determine how many people are needed for an effective security team.

The duties of each member of the team should be outlined in writing so that there will be no confusion over the duties and responsibilities of each position.

Team Leader: Responsible for the overall supervision, training, scheduling, and discipline of the security team members. Reports directly to the Elders/Deacon regarding team activities.

Assistant Team Leader: Aids the Team Leader with scheduling, supervision, and management of the security team. Secures and stores daily log records and incident reports. Asst. TL will fill in for Team Leader when that person is not available.

In the case of a large security team, specialty positions may be required; Training Director (to coordinate training and education and maintain related records) Communications Officer (oversee / PM comm gear, etc.) Legal Officer (designated Attorney for Church and Team)

The most likely scenario will be that the Priest/Pastor and the Board of Elders / Deacons will initially select the Team Leader. The Team Leader will then be responsible for nominating an Assistant Team Leader and any other positions that will need to be filled. A Team Leader, Asst. TL and a Training Director should be able to effectively screen and select team members.

Any time there is more than one team member on duty, there should be a designated Team Leader or Shift Leader. Invariably, situations will arise that will require a decision to be made regarding the security of the church or other similar matters.

"Well, everyone is equal on our team." is not a good answer. If everyone is in charge, then no one is in charge. If you cannot, or are not willing to, make a decision you are not a leader.

When the shift schedule is being made, one of the team members must be designated as the Leader, at least for that day or event. The Asst TL will typically be the one making the shift roster. When the roster is posted, someone will be the Leader. Simplify by putting a capital L next to their name.

Firearms Qualifications

If it is one thing I have learned over the years, it is that a whole lot of gun people confuse training with qualifications. I have had people say, "I've already qualified, I don't need to go to training". That is like a student saying, "I passed my 1st quarter exam for geometry. I don't need to go to anymore classes".

Training is education that gives the student the opportunity to blend what they have been taught with physical performance. Training plus practice add up to skill. You do not get skill from taking a test or "qualifying". Think of a Firearm Qualification as the exam you take after your first quarter or first semester.

With all of the above being a given, there naturally is still a place for a designated firearms qualification for Legion of Michael members. The primary reason is moral responsibility. Any armed person must carry and use their firearm in an effective and efficient manner around other people.

Another reason to establish a sanctioned firearms qualification course is to assuage the fears that elders, deacons, etc. may have about people carrying guns. By setting up a qualification and keeping records, you are demonstrating that you hold your people to a higher standard and are acting in a professional and responsible manner.

Now the question becomes, just what should be in the qual course? This question will be answered five different ways by five different gun people. A Bullseye Marksman will suggest that the course have various distances, perhaps out to fifty yards. The 3 Gun competitor will suggest a 100 round minimum course that factors in split times. The guy who only shoots soup cans in his backyard will wonder if a qual is really necessary, afterall, he's been shooting his whole life.

We want the Qualification Course to be difficult enough that the person must have skill in order to pass. However, we are not looking for an Olympic Gold Medalist either. Balance and practicality are the key. While you may have a course of fire in mind, we have included one in this text to help you get started.

The target that I would suggest is the Official Student of the Gun, Skill Maintenance Target from www.shopsotg.com. This paper target has a thoracic triangle built into the silhouette. The thoracic triangle, or TT, is the preferred impact area for rounds fired in self-defense training. The SOTG target has other features, but for the Legion of Michael Firearms Qualification we will focus on the silhouette and the triangle.

Phase 1

Target placed at 7 yards

Shooter begins with a fully loaded handgun, both hands on the gun.

On the command "Fight", the shooter fires 5 rounds at target with TT as preferred impact area

Time Limit: 20 seconds

Coach/Instructor use stopwatch on phone or second hand on watch. When the time limit is reached, the coach will announce, "Time." audibly.

*The Shooter is responsible for keeping their gun loaded at all times and will NOT be coached to reload.

Phase 2

Target placed at 3 yards

Shooter begins with a handgun held in their Dominant/Strong hand only. Non-dominant hand is held against the chest.

On the command "Fight", the shooter fires 5 rounds at the target with TT as the preferred impact area.

Time Limit: 10 seconds

*Targets will not be scored until the course of fire is completed

Phase 3

Target placed at 3 yards

Shooter begins with a handgun placed either on the range table (indoor range booth) or a plastic barrel or similar waist-height range prop. Handgun will be in ready condition.

On the command, "Fight", the shooter will pick up the handgun with their Support hand only, Dominant hand held against their chest. Shooter will fire 5 rounds into the TT area of the target.

Time Limit: 15 seconds

*Shooter will not be coached to reload handgun

Phase 4

Target placed at 5 yards

Shooter begins with a handgun placed on a range table or barrel, etc. Shooter will face 180 degrees about, with their back toward the target.

On the command "Fight", the shooter will turn around, retrieve the handgun using both hands and fire 5 rounds into the TT area of the target.

Time Limit: 10 seconds

Scoring

Coach / Instructor will retrieve the target and score it. There must be 15 shots inside of the TT area of the target for the shooter to receive a passing score. If any rounds are outside of the silhouette portion of the target, the student does not Pass.

Shooters either receive a Pass or Fail, there is no numerical score system recorded in the official records. The Firearms Qualification record sheet will note the shooter's full name, date of birth, and a notation of Pass or Fail.

If the Shooter does not pass the qualification, they will be given a remedial attempt, HOWEVER, a second Fail score will disallow the shooter from being an armed member of the Legion of Michael security team.

The shooter must attend formal and documented firearms training BEFORE they are allowed to take the Qualification test again.

*Rounds Fired after the expiration of the time limit will be deducted from the TT score.

*Any violation of the 4 Universal Firearms Safety Rules is an immediate Fail. The shooter will not be allowed to requal until documented training is completed.

Course Explanation

Many experienced and well-trained readers may view this Qual course and think "That is child's play. It's too easy." Keep in mind, this is not a test to see who the best shooter on the team might be. This a fundamental skills test to determine if the person in question is capable of handling a firearm in an effective and efficient manner.

The shooter is deliberately not coached to reload or top off their handgun because that is a part of the test. If the shooter's gun runs dry during the middle of the course of fire, they must reload it and finish within the allotted time.

Yes, the time limit is extremely generous. As long as the shooter does what they are supposed to do and keeps their gun loaded, they should not have a problem.

I would suggest that this qual course, or one very similar, be established at the very beginning of the security team formation. There will be some nice, well-meaning people who want to be a part of the team. Nonetheless, "nice" and "well-meaning" does not automatically translate to competence with a firearm. You owe a duty to the members of your congregation to ensure that the people who are designated to protect them are effective and competent gun handlers. This is not a social club, this is serious business and must be treated as such.

Anyone who wants to be on the team, but refuses to participate or balks at taking the firearms qualification will automatically disqualify him or herself. If they are not willing to go through a simple qual course, they are not serious about being a member of a team.

Again, having all members of the team go through and pass a firearms qualification course will go a long way to assuaging the fears some will have about allowing "armed men" in the church.

Chapter 8 Communications

Depending on the size of your church/church property, a team may choose portable radios for communication. Phones are too slow. A few rechargeable Motorola portable radios with earpieces should work just fine. Investment is only a few hundred dollars at most. Using an earpiece is naturally essential as you don't want the parking lot security guy blasting his "All clear" over the radio during the Lord's Prayer.

Radio Criteria

A portable radio must be:

1- Compact   2- have a Belt clip   3- be Rechargeable 4 - be Earpiece compatible.

If you want to get fancy, you can purchase the earpiece / microphone combination. Mark all radios with a number using a paint pen. Create a sign out sheet so you will know who forgot to turn in their radio and accidentally took it home.

Either a Communication Officer or the Asst TL will secure the radio logs.

The choice of specific radio brands and models is entirely up to you. Baofeng radios are inexpensive and they work. Motorola portable radios will cost more but are arguably higher quality. Midland Radio also offers compact portable radios. As I said, the choice will be made based upon your budget and preference.

Daily Logs

A simple daily log (hand-written) should be kept for each day that the security team is in place. All logs should be secured in the church offices for future referencing. Logs should be kept for regularly scheduled church services and special events (Xmas Eve, Sunrise Service, Weddings, Confirmations, etc.) As with incident reports, daily logs must be kept and secured for years as a safeguard against unwarranted and frivolous lawsuits.

Identification

If you have a large security team, you might consider a dedicated Lapel Pin for each security team member to wear. Even a small team might choose a dedicated lapel pin for esprit de corp.

Media Relations

Long before any type of incident occurs, your church should designate a spokesperson who will be responsible for fielding questions from the outside. During the aftermath of a violent attack on a house of worship, members of the media will be looking for a story. The best plan of attack is to have a spokesperson already in place.

A church attorney is the best choice for a spokesperson. Attorneys are trained in what to say and, just as importantly, what not to say on behalf of the church as an organization. Every member of the security team, as well as the board of elders/deacons, should have the church attorney's name and number. They should be instructed to forward all questions from outsiders to the attorney.

The exact same advice goes for dealing with a law enforcement investigation after any type of incident. Security team members must be educated to understand that it is not their place to give media statements and that any statements to law enforcement must be given in the presence of counsel.

Chapter 9 Situational Awareness

Situational awareness, or being a trained observer, is not necessarily something that comes naturally to most people. It is the basic condition of humans to be constantly concerned with their thoughts, wants, and desires. Most people move around in the world consumed by their own thoughts. This condition puts them at a distinct disadvantage when an unexpected stimulus occurs.

Think about driving a car. If you are driving along, totally consumed by your thoughts, worries, or concerns, and an animal, person, or another car enters your path, it is nearly impossible to react quickly enough to avoid hitting whatever appeared. Distracted drivers are a hazard on the road. Distracted security providers are useless.

Any person who desires to provide security for others must be capable of disciplining their mind and putting away all of those mental distractions, at least for a while. One of the greatest roadblocks to situational awareness is mental distraction.

In order to become a trained observer, you must look out, away from yourself and take in the world around you. Experienced hunters understand this idea. Very rarely will the game just walk out and stand still in front of you. You must be constantly aware of your surroundings and locate the clues that will expose your prey.

A trained observer is constantly monitoring their surroundings from left to right, near to far, and back again. A trained observer will deliberately minimize distractions. For the church security team member, this means not engaging directly and continuously with other church members.

"Hi, how are you? Good morning. Good to see you." are fast, polite greetings. A security team member on duty should refrain from engaging in detailed conversations with church members. If you get caught by Aunt Sarah, gently touch her shoulder and say, "It was great to see you. Will you please excuse me?"

It is important that the members of the Legion of Michael never come across to the congregation as stern, sour, or standoffish. Alway offer members a smile and a nod to acknowledge them. You want them to be glad you are there and not feel intimidated by your presence.

Another part of being a trained observer is knowing where to position yourself so as to have the greatest field of view. An elevated position is always preferable. Also, positioning your back to a wall or area where no one can approach you from the rear minimizes your need to constantly turn around.

Situational awareness also means having the ability to rapidly discern the commonplace and acceptable from the out of the ordinary, out of place, and potentially dangerous. When danger arrives, it will not do so after sending notice. You may only get one single clue that a threat is about to materialize and become a deadly attack.

In the movie, "The Bodyguard" with Kevin Costner, the very first scene involved Costner shooting and killing an assassin. When the client asks Costner's character how he knew, he responds, "I saw him washing the car." "So did I." the client responds. "They don't wash cars on the parking levels." Costner responds matter-of-factly.

Hollywood gets a lot wrong, but this one they got right. What Costner's bodyguard character pointed out was that he knew what was commonplace and acceptable, therefore he recognized the out of place and, in this case, potentially deadly. Only by knowing what is right will you be able to see what is wrong.

Another big clue is people who are not dressed appropriately for the weather. If it is 81 degrees, everyone is wearing summer clothes, and a man walks in wearing a winter coat, that is an immediate clue that something is not right with him. People with mental issues often dress inappropriately for the weather. Not all of them are dangerous, but you cannot afford to ignore what might be your only warning sign.

There is a rather famous picture of John Hinckley, moments before he shot President Ronald Reagan. The photo is a crowd shot of people happily waiting to see the new

President. Everyone in the crowd is smiling with anticipation. Everyone, that is, except Hinckley who looks stone faced, like he is about to kill someone.

Yes, all of the above mentioned examples are small, seemingly insignificant things. Nonetheless, we must realize that we may only get one small indicator that something bad is about to happen, one tiny clue that a person is about to produce a weapon and attack. Picking up on clues is what sets the trained observer apart from the average person who would never see the attack coming.

Many years ago, the late Colonel Jeff Cooper, the founder of Gunsite Academy, began teaching the color code method of mental preparedness. This system has since been widely accepted and taught by firearms instructors across the country. It was developed to easily articulate the stages of awareness and preparedness to fight that you go through in a violent encounter. I was first taught this way of thinking by John Farnam in the mid-eighties.

The first stage, or color, is White. White is a mental state of comfort. Your mind is at ease and relaxed. You are not looking for any trouble and are not prepared for any. If you were attacked in the white mindset you would be caught unaware. Most people are in white at home, in their personal comfort zone. Unfortunately, far too many people are in condition white when they leave their home and are out in public.

Yellow is the next step. In yellow you are alert and consciously aware of your surroundings. You are not looking for a specific threat and none has presented itself. This is the mental state you should always be in when moving about, especially if you are someone's protector. A protector or security provider must live in condition yellow. With some purposeful effort you can remain in mindset yellow the whole time that you are awake. Every waking moment you are prepared for an attack. Not a specific attack, but any problem that may present itself.

Condition Orange follows yellow. In this mindset you see what appears to be out of the ordinary. It may be a threat and you are aware of the possibility of a confrontation. It is now that you will consider options to deal with the possible threat. You are not yet ready to use deadly force, but you are one step closer to taking action. Here is an example of the orange mindset.

At eleven o'clock at night you stop to use an automatic teller machine. As you approach the bank machine you notice someone standing a short distance away in the doorway of the closed bank. The potential threat now becomes specific. You do not know yet that this person is an aggressor, but you mentally prepare yourself in case he is. As you mentally prepare, you may consider your options. In keeping with the example given, you may decide if this person approaches you that you will move back to your car. Maybe you have a can of OC in your pocket and you transfer it into your hand, just in case, or you place your hand near to your concealed handgun.

Finally, we have condition Red. At this point you have identified a specific threat and you have made the decision to take action. You have not yet fired your weapon, but you have given your brain permission to do so if it becomes necessary. Note: It is your brain that must give the order to fire your weapon. If the brain is not prepared to do it, your body will not react properly. In red you give yourself if / then scenarios. If they produce a weapon then I will shoot them. If they don't immediately halt when I yell "Stop!" then I will produce my weapon and aim it at them.

Some people have said that a bodyguard or security provider should just remain in condition Red all the time and view everything you see as a potential threat. Jeff Cooper understood that the human brain cannot take that kind of hyper-vigilance for very long. Remaining in a constant state of red will very quickly become mentally draining. As Cooper understood, it is far better to train your mind to rapidly progress from casual alertness to laser focused intensity on a threat.

By now it should be obvious to you why we have spent so much time discussing situational awareness and becoming a trained observer. Guns and ammunition are tools; they don't warn you of danger or provide a magic cone of invincibility. The mind is the operating system for all of your tools and that aspect deserves as much attention as the shooting drills and practice.

Chapter 10

Communing with the Flock

One negative trait that is very common in humans is the tendency to segregate into groups to the exclusion of others. Taken to the extreme we see the "us" versus "them" mentality. I have witnessed this far too often. If you want to kill off the church security team, let it become the "cool kids club" where security members start acting as if they are better than or more privileged than "regular" church members.

If the congregation starts to feel like the security team has become arrogant, aggressive toward them, confrontational, or standoffish, that will be the beginning of the end of the team. It won't be long before the elders or deacons abolish the team.

One of my many mentors, I cannot recall which one, explained to me the idea of the Sheep, the Wolf, and the Sheepdog. The sheep or flock do not live in fear of the wolf. They never see the wolf unless he attacks. If the sheepdog is doing his job, the wolf will stay away. The sheep fear the sheepdog, not the wolf. They fear the sheepdog because he is alway there. He barks to keep them together or in a formation and he bears a resemblance to the wolf.

People are the same way when it comes to the presence of armed security or guards. They do not truly fear the wolf or the killer, because they never have to see the killer, particularly if security does its job. But, the people/sheep do see the sheepdog/security. He has a gun, like the killer, but they don't see the killer, they see the guard. They fear the armed guard more than a faceless, unseen armed killer. It is irrational and illogical, but it remains a fact in many cases.

Thinking back to my time as a professional bodyguard, I saw more than one agent get relieved and sent packing because the client's wife or kids did not like them. It was not that these people were unqualified to be protectors. It was that they somehow rubbed someone the wrong way. The fact that this situation was surrounded by feelings did not make it any less real. Imagine that the congregation is your billionaire client's wife. If the wife doesn't like you, for whatever reason, you will not be around very long.

Whether you have a current security team or a looking to start one, there needs to be an openness or transparency to the group. Those in the church who feel excluded from "the club" may harbor animosity towards the team and its leader. We want to avoid this to the greatest extent that we can.

Good food always brings people together. One of the suggestions that I have offered many times is for the church security team to organize either some kind of spaghetti dinner, potluck, pancake brunch, whatever. This is where having an auxiliary or helpful and cheerful wives can come in.

Stay away from the doom and gloom, "people are coming to kill us" kind of talk. Everyone in the congregation gets the news on their phones or TV. They are aware of the ongoing attacks on houses of worship in the United States. This is not the time to sell them on fear.

This is the time to demonstrate that you have a plan besides "be scared".

Give them the pickle. Organize a free training event around the dinner. After everyone has had their fill, give a talk and demonstration about any simple, but useful topic. The "Stop the Bleed" type programs are vogue now and people should recognize the value. A forty-five minute to an hour long explanation and demonstration about how to stop heavy bleeding using a tourniquet or pressure dressing is a great place to start.

Remember, offer solutions, not problems. Those who came to the dinner and sit through a quick stop the bleed class should all come away with a serious warm fuzzy feeling about this whole church security team business. They ate good food, which always puts people in a happy mood. Then you gave them some valuable information, free of charge, to demonstrate your dedication to keeping them safe from harm. All this without a powerpoint on church shootings.

Armed Parishioners

In many states it is perfectly legal for armed citizens to carry concealed firearms to church. Some people see the idea of an armed congregation being at odds with an organized church security team. I see it very differently.

First of all, the idea that the presence of a security team would justify a disarmed congregation is folly. These people will spend an hour or two at church. Are you going to provide armed escorts to and from worship services? Of course not.

Some congregations will push back against the idea of a security team because, "we can all carry guns, if we want to". By this point in time you should be fully armed to take down that empty argument. Professional security is about far more than just having a gun.

If you are in a circumstance where your church has formed a security team and many people in the congregation regularly carry concealed firearms, the best approach is to be an ally, not an adversary. Once more, if your team becomes the exclusive, cool guy club, it will not last long. You need the flock on your side.

Following the previous example, I would approach the armed church member situation by organizing a get-together and inviting everyone who carries a concealed firearm, and even those who are contemplating doing so, to attend. Share a meal or at very least coffee and snacks. Put together a training course and be sure that it focuses on class participation.

This might be a good opportunity to bring in some type of recognized subject matter expert. If your Sheriff is a pro-liberty person, ask them to come and give a talk about Justifiable Use of Force or something similar. If you have not yet done the Stop the Bleed trauma training, this is a good place for that. Keep in mind that training for the gun carriers should be more detailed and comprehensive than what you might give to the curious church member.

When the training program is over, thank everyone for their participation and reward them with a lapel pin that signifies that they are a graduate of whatever program you have put on for them. The pin should have some kind of significance.

For instance, the archangel Raphael is considered the patron saint of healing. If you have graduates of a detailed trauma class, a Raphael lapel pin would seem very appropriate. When you present the pin, be sure to highlight the significance and how they have earned it.

When people have earned a pin, badge, etc. they are far more likely to wear it proudly than if it were just given to them for doing nothing. I proudly wear the Eagle, Globe, and Anchor symbol of the United States Marine Corps because I earned it.

The training and the lapel pins serve numerous purposes. First, they establish you as an ally to the armed church members, a friend and team member, not an adversary. When these armed church members wear their pins proudly on their church clothing, your team will know that they are armed parishioners who have taken training and have demonstrated the moral responsibility of improving themselves.

If you choose to run the armed parishioners through a Beyond the Band Aid / Trauma medicine course, their lapel pin will mark them as a trained medical responder. In the event of a traumatic medical emergency, if a Legion member sees a person wearing that pin, they can call on them for help, knowing that the person with the pin took the trauma training.

Also, invariably, people will inquire of the pin wearers as to the significance of the symbol. When the pin wearer proudly recalls how they earned the pin, that will inspire others to want to be a part of that group. Even if these curious people do not ever take training or carry a gun to church, they will know that the Legion of Michael security team is a well-organized, professional-acting group and they are present to aid and assist the entire church body.

This basic training for armed church members is also a good avenue to recruit new members for your formal security team. Having already witnessed their behavior in the basic class, you will have a strong idea of whether or not they would be a good fit for the team.

Chapter 11 Post-Incident

We have discussed the tools and training that we may be called upon to put to use to stop any type of unwarranted attack on the church body. Your primary mission is to stop the threat from causing harm to the absolute best of your ability. Priority #1 is Win the Fight.

After the physical fight against a human attacker(s) has been won, you still have work to do. The most time sensitive issue is dealing with the injuries of good guys. Just because you won the gunfight does not mean that innocent/friendly people were not injured. Hopefully no good guy was harmed, but we cannot rely on luck. The moment it is safe to do so, start checking for injuries. This includes yourself, as you may be injured and not realize it. Adrenaline is stronger than morphine when it comes to masking pain.

As soon as the lethal threat has been dealt with, we must deal with any victims of the attack. All Church Security Team members should be trained to deal with Life-threatening Traumatic Injuries.

The Top 3 Preventable Death Injuries are as follows:

1- Massive Hemorrhage from the limbs - solution = Tourniquet
2- Loss of Airway - solution = Head tilt / NPA
3- Tension Pneumothorax - solution = Chest Seal / Chest Decomp Needle

Emergency services should be contacted during this phase. Give the dispatcher clear and concise information, but keep it brief. They don't need to know what you had for breakfast. If you were directly involved in the incident, you will still be under the effects of the adrenaline dump.

Tell the dispatcher that there are armed good guys on the scene. Describe the bad guy(s) and request medical attention for any victims. Even if only that the attacker(s) is injured, an ambulance should be sent. Keep your communication with the police dispatcher simple, short, and absolutely to the point. If the scene is secure, tell the dispatcher that someone will be in the parking lot to guide them. Give an exact description, including clothing, of the good guy who will meet responding officers. This person must not have a gun or any weapon in their hands.

Physical Effects of Adrenaline

- Blood rushes to the large muscle groups, increase strength but loss of fine motor skills
- Pain and injury is masked (adrenaline is 60x more powerful than morphine)
- Heart rate / pulse increases dramatically
- Auditory exclusion (hard to hear)
- Tunnel vision (peripheral vision diminished)
- Dilated pupils
- Increased respiration

Mental / Emotional Effects of Adrenaline

- Mood amplified, Post-shooting Euphoria (Elated to be alive)
- Time/Space distortion (you will not be able to count the rounds you fire)
- Loss of Memory / Distortion of Events (remembering things out of order)

- Denial response (refuse to believe)
- Post-Adrenaline Crash (going from very high to very low)

Understand this, when responding officers arrive, they only need you to answer a few questions; Who goes to the hospital? Who goes to the morgue? Who goes to jail? That's about it. They don't need to know what you ate for breakfast, what books you read, your favorite color, your preferred handgun and ammo. All of that can come later.

Your cooperation should lend to answering the first three questions about hospital, morgue, and jail. Post-traumatic shock and adrenaline can, and will, make you say incorrect things and cause you to make honest mistakes that can be damning later on.

One of the biggest errors people will make, in the post-attack adrenaline dump, is to give a statement as to how many rounds they fired. Innumerable police officers have said they thought they fired "x" rounds but really fired "y". After a deadly force encounter, police officers have said, "I fired two or three times" and it turned out there were eight empty cases on the ground around them. It is not that they are lying, it is the very real effects of a traumatic event.

Go back to our first three questions; hospital, morgue, jail. Does it matter, when blood is still wet on the ground, the exact round count fired? No, it does not. We have until the end of time to figure that out.

Returning to our discussion of who says what to whom, all security team members must be trained to ask for the presence of counsel before giving any kind of formal statement. Please do not take this as advice to stonewall or refuse to speak to responding officers. When they say "Who is hurt and needs an ambulance?" Tell them and show them. "Where is the gunman?" Tell them and show them.

"How many people are on your team? Who are they and what are all of their names?" Response, "I will be happy to answer all of your questions in the presence of our church attorney."

Responding officers need to know who the bad guys/attackers are and where they are. They need to know who the victims are and how many of them need help. Everything else is just details that can be figured out after the wounded are cared for and the criminal attackers are removed from the scene to the jail, hospital, or the morgue.

First Aid for Killers

Some people have offered that to render medical aid to the killer or wannabe killer after they have been neutralized by armed security is the Christian thing to do. To that statement I would say "yes" they will get first aid treatment after we have determined that they are no longer a threat and all of the innocent people have been given treatment. I am not putting a tourniquet on a murderer until I am one-hundred percent positive that no innocent person needs it to save their life.

Remember our FBI Miami scenario. Even people who are shot and have non-survivable wounds can still be deadly. If they are moving and have access to a weapon, they are still dangerous even if they are on the ground and leaking.

Speaking of leaking, the blood of a killer is just as likely to have bloodborne pathogens as it is not. Hepatitis B, HIV, etc. can all be picked up through bodily fluid. Every trauma kit should have disposable gloves. The point is this, exercise extreme caution when it comes to rendering aid to the attacker who moments earlier wanted to harm the innocent church members.

Chapter 12

Other Safety Considerations

Any professional security provider should understand that there is far more to the job than standing around with a gun waiting for something to happen. As a matter of fact, if you do your job well, the likelihood that something tragic occurs will diminish.

One of many lessons that a bodyguard must learn is one of environmental control, or controlling the environment in which your client is living and working. This is not so difficult if we are talking about a private person or private property. The greatest challenge to professional security comes when dealing with a client who is accessible to others or in an area that is open to the public.

"Open to the Public" is the name of the game when it comes to houses of worship. We want sinners to come inside, repent, and be saved. We want the people of the congregation to commune together. *"For where two or three*

gather in my name, there am I with them."
Matthew 18:20

This is a challenge for your Legion of Michael team. How do you keep the church open to all, while at the same time be on guard for evil men who would harm the worshippers? If it was easy, everyone would do it.

One area to give close consideration are the entrances to the sanctuary. Thinking back to my church in Detroit, Michigan when I was a kid, there were probably four different ways for people to enter the main sanctuary. There was, of course, the main entrance area and even that had a front set of doors and a side door. Every place that people can enter your area of responsibility is a concern.

If your church has numerous front, back, and side entrances, you may need to conduct an assessment and determine if it is truly necessary for them all to be open to outside traffic. Fire exits, naturally, must remain accessible, but they can be one way; out only.

Another area of control and concern is the parking lot. A church parking area is obvious to all who care to look, and a potential target for evil men. Depending on your mission and manpower, you may want to dedicate one team member to being outside and monitoring the parking area and the primary walking route to the church. Afterall, if evil men wish to harm your flock, they have to get in somehow. It is far better to catch them outside than inside.

When conducting a survey of the entire church grounds, look at it as if you were trying to enter the building without being detected. Is there a side door that is always left unlocked? Could a man or men get inside without your team seeing them? If so, you have a potential problem. Don't make it easy. If someone with evil intent targets your church, you want to make them work for it. Be the hard target, not the soft one.

Your facility survey is also a great time to check the fire extinguishers, their placement and charge status. You cannot put out a fire with your Glock. Every person on your team should be able to move immediately to the closest fire extinguisher without having to look around and wonder.

Does your church have an AED (automatic electronic defibrillator)? If so, where is it located? If it is locked in the deacon's office so it doesn't get stolen, that is the wrong answer. You might think, no one would be so stupid as to lock up a life-saving piece of equipment. You'd be amazed.

When I was working as a police officer, our department used to provide security for the football and basketball games for the local high school. During one basketball game I was walking in the main hall of the high school and noticed that the AED case mounted on the wall was empty. I brought that up to my Sergeant and he made inquiries.

It turned out that the AED (a life-saving piece of medical gear) had been taken out and was locked in the principal's office. The explanation we were given to that insanity was, "Those things are expensive. We didn't want to risk it being stolen." Yeah, that happened.

The next obvious question is; do all of your team members know how to use the AED? Don't tell me that the instructions are in the box. Every local firehouse should be able to run you through a one hour "how to" course with the AED. Those guys get grant money to buy and teach people how to use them. Take advantage of the resources that are available to you.

Chapter 13 Leadership

Here is your lagniappe, a little something extra. If you are putting together, or if you have already established, a Church Security team you have assumed a leadership role. Even if you do not want to be in charge of anything, the fact that you are concerned with, and focused on, keeping your congregation safe puts you in a leadership position.

People will eventually look to you to set the example. Other folks will come to you for advice. Without a doubt, the members of your church will be watching you and observing how you interact with others. This is a great time to focus on leadership training.

During this chapter I am going to dip back into the well of knowledge and information that I learned to drink from nearly thirty years ago; United States Marine Corps Leadership training. Back when I was in the Corps, shortly after a Marine became a Lance Corporal they were groomed to become a Non-Commissioned Officer (NCO). In addition to being mentored by experienced NCO's, young Marines were strongly encouraged to complete Marine Corps Institute courses for advancement. One MCI course required to achieve the rank of Corporal was "Leadership."

Marine Corps Leadership Traits

When I was a member of the Marine Detachment stationed aboard the aircraft carrier USS Forrestal, the ladder (stairs for civilians) that lead out of our berthing area was painted Marine Corp red and on each rung was a single word painted in yellow (we didn't have crimson and gold paint). Fourteen words were visible every time we ascended the ladder. Those words were the fourteen leadership traits.

Rather than paraphrase the leadership traits or attempt to restate them, I will instead offer them to you verbatim. Take a moment to digest each and every trait and consider where you are on your journey.

The fourteen leadership traits are qualities of thought and action which, if demonstrated in daily activities, help Marines earn the respect, confidence, and loyal cooperation of other Marines. It is extremely important that you understand the meaning of each leadership trait and how to develop it, so you know what goals to set as you work to become a good leader and a good follower.

JUSTICE

Definition: Justice is defined as the practice of being fair and consistent. A just person gives consideration to each side of a situation and bases rewards or punishments on merit.

Suggestions for Improvement: Be honest with yourself about why you make a particular decision. Avoid favoritism. Try to be fair at all times and treat all things and people in an equal manner.

JUDGMENT

Definition: Judgment is your ability to think about things clearly, calmly, and in an orderly fashion so that you can make good decisions.

Suggestions for Improvement: You can improve your judgment if you avoid making rash decisions. Approach problems with a common sense attitude.

DEPENDABILITY

Definition: Dependability means that you can be relied upon to perform your duties properly. It means that you can be trusted to complete a job. It is the willing and voluntary support of the policies and orders of the chain of command.

Dependability also means consistently putting forth your best effort in an attempt to achieve the highest standards of performance.

Suggestions for Improvement: You can increase your dependability by forming the habit of being where you're supposed to be on time, by not making excuses and by carrying out every task to the best of your ability regardless of whether you like it or agree with it.

INITIATIVE

Definition: Initiative is taking action even though you haven't been given orders. It means meeting new and unexpected situations with prompt action. It includes using resourcefulness to get something done without the normal material or methods being available to you.

Suggestions for Improvement: To improve your initiative, work on staying mentally and physically alert. Be aware of things that need to be done and then to do them without having to be told.

DECISIVENESS

Definition: Decisiveness means that you are able to make good decisions without delay. Get all the facts and weigh them against each other. By acting calmly and quickly, you should arrive at a sound decision. You announce your decisions in a clear, firm, professional manner.

Suggestions for Improvement: Practice being positive in your actions instead of acting half-heartedly or changing your mind on an issue.

TACT

Definition: Tact means that you can deal with people in a manner that will maintain good relations and avoid problems. It means that you are polite, calm, and firm.

Suggestions for Improvement: Begin to develop your tact by trying to be courteous and cheerful at all times. Treat others as you would like to be treated.

INTEGRITY

Definition: Integrity means that you are honest and truthful in what you say or do. You put honesty, sense of duty, and sound moral principles above all else.

Suggestions for Improvement: Be absolutely honest and truthful at all times. Stand up for what you believe to be right.

ENTHUSIASM

Definition: Enthusiasm is defined as a sincere interest and exuberance in the performance of your duties. If you are enthusiastic, you are optimistic, cheerful, and willing to accept the challenges.

Suggestions for Improvement: Understanding and belief in your mission will add to your enthusiasm for your job. Try to understand why even uninteresting jobs must be done.

BEARING

Definition: Bearing is the way you conduct and carry yourself. Your manner should reflect alertness, competence, confidence, and control.

Suggestions for Improvement: To develop bearing, you should hold yourself to the highest standards of personal conduct. Never be content with meeting only the minimum requirements.

UNSELFISHNESS

Definition: Unselfishness means that you avoid making yourself comfortable at the expense of others. Be considerate of others. Give credit to those who deserve it.

Suggestions for Improvement: Avoid using your position or rank for personal gain, safety, or pleasure at the expense of others. Be considerate of others.

COURAGE

Definition: Courage is what allows you to remain calm while recognizing fear. Moral courage means having the inner strength to stand up for what is right and to accept blame when something is your fault. Physical courage means that you can continue to function effectively when there is physical danger present.

Suggestions for Improvement: You can begin to control fear by practicing self-discipline and calmness. If you fear doing certain things required in your daily life, force yourself to do them until you can control your reaction.

KNOWLEDGE

Definition: Knowledge is the understanding of a science or art. Knowledge means that you have acquired information and that you understand people. Your knowledge should be broad, and in addition to knowing your job, you should know your unit's policies and keep up with current events.

Suggestions for Improvement: Suggestions for Improvement: Increase your knowledge by remaining alert. Listen, observe, and find out about things you don't understand. Study field manuals and other military literature.

LOYALTY

Definition: Loyalty means that you are devoted to your country, the Corps, and to your seniors, peers, and subordinates. The motto of our Corps is Semper Fidelis!, (Always Faithful). You owe unwavering loyalty up and down the chain of command, to seniors, subordinates, and peers.

Suggestions for Improvement: To improve your loyalty you should show your loyalty by never discussing the problems of the Marine Corps or your unit with outsiders. Never talk about seniors unfavorably in front of your subordinates. Once a decision is made and the order is given to execute it, carry out that order willingly as if it were your own.

ENDURANCE

Definition: Endurance is the mental and physical stamina that is measured by your ability to withstand pain, fatigue, stress, and hardship. For example, enduring pain during a conditioning march in order to improve stamina is crucial in the development of leadership.

Suggestions for Improvement: Develop your endurance by engaging in physical training that will strengthen your body. Finish every task to the best of your ability by forcing yourself to continue when you are physically tired and your mind is sluggish.

Because it is important to always be able to remember the basic leadership traits, the acronym "J.J. DID TIE BUCKLE" is used. Each letter in the acronym corresponds to the first letter of one of the traits. By remembering the acronym, you will be better able to recall the traits.

Parting Thoughts

Naturally I would not expect you to master each and every leadership trait in one session. Instead, what I would challenge you to do is to take a two week, or fourteen day, challenge. Each morning before you begin your day read one Marine Corps leadership trait, write it down or type it into your phone. Hell, send yourself a text reminding you of that day's trait. I might even be able to convince Jarrad to send you a reminder each morning.

As you progress through each day look for ways or areas where you might be able to apply the trait of the day. By the end of two weeks you should be on your way toward self-improvement and understanding the path to leadership.

Chapter 14   Final Thoughts

Some might offer an opinion that church security should be much simpler than I have outlined during these pages. The truth is that everything is simple and easy until something unexpected occurs. Think of the untrained gun carrier like the self-taught motorcycle rider. As long as the conditions are perfect and nothing unexpected ever happens, both of them will be just fine.

However, when trouble comes unexpectedly or an obstacle appears in the road, the untrained gun carrier, like the self-taught rider, default to the level of training they have mastered. In this case, they have mastered no training and they are an accident or tragedy waiting to happen.

Many police officers will go for years without having to draw their gun in self-defense. Just because that statement is true does not mean that they can just ignore firearms training and practice.

When I was in the police academy, one of my instructors advised us that the reason we needed to train so diligently, and dedicate our minds and bodies to practice, was because one day we might be called upon to use that skill. The instructor went on to elaborate. "You will have mere seconds to decide and act. However, the same decision that took you seconds will be examined again and again, for hours, days, even weeks by people who were not even there."

Someday you will be called upon to defend your actions. From an Earthly perspective, you may be required to stand before a judge and twelve of your peers to explain your actions. From a more important standpoint, one day you will stand in front of your Maker to give account for your actions. I don't know about you, but I do not want to stand before God the Father and explain that, while He gave me the mind and body to be a protector of the innocent, I decided it was not worth my time or effort.

Remember the Parable of the Talents. If God has given you the talent, the skill and ability to be the defender of his innocent sheep, but you squander that talent is that not a sin? When you meet your Maker, and you will, will he say to you "Well done my good and faithful servant" or will you be cast out into the darkness where there is weeping and gnashing of teeth?

My prayer for everyone who reads this book is that God will bless you with the strength and courage to make the most of the talents which He has bestowed upon you. If your talent is that of a protector, go forward and embrace that talent and protect his flock.

For more Training and to bond with other like minded individuals, please go to:

www.LegionofMichael.com

Other inspirational and motivational books from Paul Markel include;

Faith and the Patriot: A Belief Worth Fighting For

The Intolerant Christian: Examining the Persecution of Faithful Christians in the United States of American